Harry the Bully Blocker

Evelyn M. Field OAM

Dedication

To my grandchildren: Mia, Eli and Layla.

And to Harry and Buffy, my two special Papillons, who spent years teaching me about therapy, social connectivity and bullying.

First published in 2021 in Australia

Copyright © Evelyn M. Field, 2021

The moral rights of the author have been asserted.

All rights reserved. Except as permitted under the Australian Copyright Act 1968 (for example, a fair dealing for the purposes of study, research, criticism or review), no part of this book may be reproduced, stored in a retrieval system, communicated or transmitted in any form or by any means without prior written permission.

All inquiries should be made to the author.

The material in this publication is of the nature of general comment only, and does not represent professional advice. It is not intended to provide specific guidance for particular circumstances and it should not be relied on as the basis for any decision to take action or not take action on any matter which it covers. Readers should obtain professional advice where appropriate, before making any such decision. To the maximum extent permitted by law, the author and publisher disclaim all responsibility and liability to any person, arising directly or indirectly from any person taking or not taking action based on the information in this publication.

Illustrations by Adrian Osborne

Design by saso.creative

Text edited and project managed by Sean Doyle of Lynk Manuscript Assessment Service

Author photo by Sonia Payes

Harry the Bully Blocker audiobook: reading by Kaaren Champion, music composition and sound production by Paul Archer Music (www.paularchermusic.com.au).

10 9 8 7 6 5 4 3 2 1

978-0-9942791-8-7

Advance praise for this book

'Harry is a great story with a happy ending. It can teach you how to stand up to bullies when they are being mean to you.'

Eli, aged 9.

'Ruth seemed to engage a lot in the scenarios and was able to "block" and "retort". Mike is a different kind of learner. He acted disengaged and did not want to participate in the scenarios. I think some of it was a bit close to home for him and I know he has been bullied before, even as recently as this week.'

Mother of two.

'I love how this book teaches kids that there is a really easy way to stop bullies. And I really enjoy that it's not a human and it's a dog. Harry is very adorable.'

Stephanie, aged 10.

'Dogs are great teachers, in times of fun and sadness. Their comfort is what gets many people out of bed each day. We laugh or cry at their antics. Dogs as therapy helps everyone. [This is] a lovely rhyming book that will be easy to read with children.'

Vivien, Stephanie's mother.

'Harry is super cute and would be helpful for primary-school-aged children.'

Judith David, Clinical psychologist.

'This book uses the art of poetry to cleverly help children understand the experience of bullying, and presents a way forward for children who are either bullying or being bullied.'

David Opat, Child psychologist and Vice-Principal.

'In a nutshell, Evelyn Field teaches children the importance of "not reacting" to bullying behaviour. The students I share this approach with find it challenging but effective. *Harry the Bully Blocker* is full of rhyming quips and tips to help children embrace this idea and implement other strategies related to bullying. The ideas presented in the book can be especially useful when read together with an adult. Evelyn has also included a whole section of guiding questions adults can use to engage children and support the book's teachings.'

Biteena Frazier, School Counsellor, Yew Chung International School of Shanghai.

'Harry is so relatable, and Evelyn's ability — through this story — to empower through the real and practical skill of navigating bullying transcends all age limitations.'

Workplace Bullying Survivor, aged 56.

'Jack [aged 12] was bullied in six schools and is going to his seventh school next year following an overdose. He didn't get help from the school or the psychiatrist. However, while he was reading Harry, his demeanour and expression changed: slowly he began looking positive and empowered. He liked the rhyming and pictures.'

Jack's father, passenger on P.O. Jewel.

Author Note

Harry the Bully Blocker can help anyone who feels like a bullied child learn how to block bullies and build important social skills. It can be used by parents, teachers and therapists alike.

Please beware that it may trigger very painful feelings for the bullied child.

Contents

Chapter 1	1
Chapter 2	5
Chapter 3	9
Chapter 4	15
Chapter 5	23
Chapter 6	29
Chapter 7	41
Exercises	51
Notes for parents and teachers for involving children in further discussion	59
Acknowledgements	60

Chapter One

Verse 1

Harry is a Papillon -
That's French for 'butterfly'.
He's a small and handsome dog
And a gentle sort of guy.

Verse 2

Children love to cuddle him.
We know this without doubt.
And Harry likes it too because
His little tongue peeps out.

Verse 3

If kids are scared or worried,
Harry sits up on their lap.
When they both feel relaxed,
He drifts off for a nap.

Chapter One

Verse 4

Buffy is his older sister.
She has a feisty face,
And a curly tail,
She is the boss at their place.

Verse 5

She is friendly and confident
Caring and brave.
The two dogs get along okay
But she doesn't always behave.

Verse 6

Now Harry has a social worry:
He is very shy.
He is scared of everything
And he doesn't know why.

Verse 7

The secret is in Harry's mouth:
He was born with two less teeth.
He feels that something isn't right
And this gives him constant grief.

Verse 8

He has to eat quite slowly,
Which means Buffy takes his food.
This leaves him feeling hungry
And in a grumpy mood.

Verse 9

Although some dogs like Harry
And come to him to play,
He thinks they are pretending
And pushes them away!

Chapter Two

Verse 1

Some dogs say mean words to him
If he comes too near.
It's not that they hate Harry,
They just like to see his fear.

Verse 2

If he gets angry and fights back,
It makes the bullying worse.
He's sad that life is so unfair—
It feels like he's been cursed.

Verse 3

They call him 'fat' and 'dumb',
They say he's 'ugly' or 'a girl'.
They push him around in circles.
Harry's in a sickening whirl.

Verse 4

Some other dogs, they run and hide
If Harry walks their way.
If he sees them, they growl and shout,
'No one likes you. Go away.'

Chapter Two

Verse 5

Some dogs pick on Harry -
They say he has a different face.
That's dumb: there's nothing wrong with
Coming from another race.

Verse 6

Harry's face and body change
When he feels attacked.
This threatens bullies, who are scared.
They want to pay him back.

Verse 7

Harry feels quite confused.
He doesn't know why they're mean.
He thinks, 'I've done nothing to them.'
He doesn't know what they've seen.

Verse 8

He doesn't know what he should do.
He thinks his fears don't show.
He says, 'I don't care if I'm bullied.'
But dogs see his fright, and know.

Verse 9

Older dogs say, 'Toughen up',
But they don't tell him how.
They can't explain what he should do
So their advice is useless now.

Verse 10

Poor Harry needs someone to say,
'Here are some reasons why dogs bully,
And when you learn the right way,
Dogs stop and respect you fully.'

Verse 11

Like every dog, he makes a mess,
Does silly things and then gets blamed.
He's already sad and lonely;
This makes him feel more ashamed.

Chapter Three

Verse 1

He tried to tell his parents
But they had a bigger problem.
He needed love and sympathy
But didn't want to bother them.

Verse 2

He went outside to clear his head
And realised he had to pee.
He went to his favourite spot
Under the big, white camellia tree.

Chapter Three

Verse 3

Then he lay down, slept and dreamt -
Not of mean dogs or boring teachers
But of something truly magical:
Wild but friendly, caring creatures.

Verse 4

First came Mia, a
 wise meerkat.
Harry grunted and
 groaned.
'Why make these sad
 sounds?' she asked.
'Some dogs are mean
 to me,' he moaned.

Verse 5

Mia knows life is a puzzle.
You need to get every fact,
Then think and plan what you will do
Before you go ahead and act.

Verse 6

Harry sensed that she could help.
'What do those dogs want you to do?'
She asked, looking him in the eye,
'When they're mean and bully you?'

Verse 7

This question startled young Harry,
Whose eyebrows rose and ears wiggled.
He gasped for air and looked at her.
She smiled when his nose jiggled!

Verse 8

'When dogs bully,' Mia went on,
'How do they want you to react?
Do you walk away, do "nothing"?
Get upset or get angry back?

Verse 9

'Do you think you're clever if you say,
"Stop, I don't like it, you fool"?
Or think it's over if you tell
A teacher at your puppy school?'

Chapter Three

Verse 10

'Well,' Harry said, 'I've tried them all.
I show my worries and my fear.
I get upset and angry back,
Tell the teacher ... and I disappear.'

Verse 11

She said, 'You become their target
When you do some of these things.
You give them what they want
When they see your hurt feelings.'

Verse 12

A strange look now crossed Mia's face,
Her voice grew strong and snappy.
'Tell me, pup, why do you want
To make these bullies happy?'

Verse 13

Harry looked at her in total shock.
His jaw dropped, his eyes went wide.
He was stunned to hear these words.
He shook his head from side to side.

Verse 14

He grunted, 'I don't know why.'
Mia nodded and sighed.
'Bullies smell distress, so you must stop
Feeling so worried inside.

Verse 15

'When you grow quiet, pale or blush,
Their gut instinct spies anger or fear.
They know your stresses all too well
And fight back as if danger is near.

Verse 16

'When you get angry or shed tears
You show them what they feel inside,
Like a video of their deepest fears
And worries they want to hide!'

Verse 17

Harry felt strange and very surprised.
When he trashed this false belief,
He would surprise the bullies
And he would feel a great relief!

Chapter Four

Verse 1

Mia said, 'Let's take a walk. Maybe
We'll learn another way
To feel strong inside ourselves
And block those bullies every day.'

Verse 2

As they walked
   along a path
They met an owl
   called Ollie.
He was kind and
   old and wise
And looked like
   a toy dolly.

Verse 3

Ollie asked, 'What brings you here?'
Mia said, 'Harry makes bullies glad.
He doesn't want to, but he usually
Gets angry, scared or sad.

Chapter Four

Verse 4

'We are looking for ideas
So Harry can find the right actions
To help him block bullies
By changing his reactions.'

Verse 5

Ollie smiled. 'I look people in the eye.
I don't want to be too hasty –
I make sure they are kind and friendly
And avoid those who are nasty.'

Verse 6

Mia nodded. 'Good advice,' she said.
'Thanks, Mr Owl,' said Harry.
'His words will help,' said Mia.
'And they're not heavy to carry.

Verse 7

'There's lots of ways to show your fear,'
She added. 'Bounce like a yoyo,
Jiggle like a teabag,
Slouch like a couch potato.

Verse 8

'Watch people closely, like Ollie said.
Are they friendly to everyone?
Or do they have a plan: are they
Nice to most but mean to some?'

Verse 9

They took shelter under a shady tree
To hide from the sun's glare.
Mia was delighted to see
Gerry the giraffe standing there.

Chapter Four

Verse 10

Gerry said, 'When I stand up straight,
I breathe more deeply,
I feel more confident
And I speak more clearly.

Verse 11

'That works for me but still, you know,
Whenever I meet a stranger,
Like every creature in the world,
I check for signs of danger.'

Verse 12

As they walked along, they saw a prickly thing.
It was a young echidna in disguise.
His name was Eddie,, a friendly chap
Who Harry didn't recognise.

Verse 13

Eddie said, 'When I'm scared, I curl up
In a ball to hide my pain,
But you deal with your worries
By using your smart brain.

Verse 14

'You need to look cool and calm,
Hide what you feel inside.
Don't make bullies happy!
Let these words be your guide.

Verse 15

'If dogs attack you physically,
Or abuse you on social media,
You should report and block them.
Don't put up with that behaviour.

Chapter Four

Verse 16

'If they do an "eye roll", ask them,
"What's wrong with your eye?
Have you just got out of bed,
Or have you caught a filthy fly?"

Verse 17

'If a group wants to exclude you
And says, "You don't belong",
Forget them and find nicer dogs
Who say, "You want to come along?"

Verse 18

'Some dogs are friendly one day, mean the next.
Leave those who keep changing their mind.
Let them have their silly moods:
Find others who are true and kind.

Verse 19

'Dogs at camp like to play games,
Which they call "just jokes".
They say it's fun, but they know
It really hurts some folks.

Verse 20

'Some dogs believe their breed is best –
They bully if you're not the same.
So remember, always hide your stress.
Being a target is an awful "game".

Verse 21

'Some bullies attack in a group.
You can't face them on your own.
You must ask someone for help –
Don't deal with it alone.'

Verse 22

Harry nodded. 'I can play with other dogs
But I'll be more aware
Of how they treat each other –
If they smirk, stare or don't care.'

Verse 23

'Yes,' said Eddie, 'That's the way.
True friends will protect you,
And stand by you if you're upset,
Like really good mates do.'

Chapter Five

Verse 1

They said goodbye to Eddie
And soon reached the dog park.
Dogs were running and sniffing everywhere
And having a great bark.

Chapter Five

Verse 2

Mia said, 'Harry needs help with bullies.'
Eli asked, 'What teases do they use?'
Eli, a schnoodle with curly hair,
Wanted to share some useful clues.

Verse 3

Harry said, 'They call me ugly, stupid and fat.'
Clever Eli smiled. 'OK, is any of that true?
I don't think it is, because
That's not how I see you.

Verse 4

'Tell me,' Eli went on, 'Are you stupid?'
Harry said, 'I'm really good at farting.
I'm not so good at eating
But quite good at barking.'

Verse 5

'And are you very fat?'
'A bit. Our food is oh-so yummy.
It's homemade and tastes so good –
I love to fill my tummy!'

Verse 6

Eli said, 'You make bullies happy
When you show them you're upset.
You're not fat or dumb, but still
You need a safer mindset.

Verse 7

'Work out which teases are true or not.
Find someone you trust to show
How to understand the reasons why
These stupid words upset you so.

Verse 8

'Whatever type of tease it is,
Hide what you feel inside.
To help protect yourself,
Use simple comebacks as a guide.

Chapter Five

Verse 9

'Practise retorts to block them, like:
"And?", "Thanks", "Nobody's perfect,
But you know, I'm pretty close,
And getting there is my next project."

Verse 10

'You can change some painful teases,
Such as if they call you "fat".
If it's true and you don't like it,
Exercise and healthy food can help that.

Verse 11

'If they say, "You can't hit a ball",
You can agree and then say,
"I'm getting a lot better,
Practising with Dad every day."

Verse 12

'If they tease you with mean stuff like,
"No-one likes you", "Go away", "You're dumb",
Don't worry, use a practised reply,
And make sure you don't look glum.'

Verse 13

Eli said, 'You're so good-looking –
You're no prickly hedgehog.
With a little bit of grooming,
You could be a show dog!

Verse 14

'No wonder they are jealous
Of the talents you possess.
And if you use them wisely,
They'll bring future success.

Verse 15

'Find easy replies and comebacks,
Role-play with your family.
Or practise using video
Until they pop out naturally.'

Chapter Six

Verse 1

Harry was still feeling confused.
'How does this really work?' he said.
Mia answered, 'OK, you're not sure?
Just consider this instead.

Verse 2

'When you reached the dog park today
And tried to join our group,
I was mean and bullied you
To stand beside dog poop.

Chapter Six

Verse 3

'You looked at me politely
As you didn't want to fail,
Then ignored my bullying and
Blocked me with your bushy tail!

Verse 4

'It's exactly the same with words:
If you give a neutral reply
When someone's mean to you,
It's like hitting the bull's-eye.

Verse 5

'When you block others politely,
They feel confused and stuck.
They don't know what to do or say,
And become dumbstruck.

Verse 6

'Their eyes open wide, their jaw drops,
Their head moves up and down,
They do a quick headshake
And their face looks like a clown.

Verse 7

'When you take away their power,
They will feel surprised
And become embarrassed.
You need respect, they realise.

Verse 8

'Everyone knows that being
Embarrassed is a real pain.
You can be sure that they won't try
To bully you again!

Verse 9

'Do you know what happens
When you block this pest?
Others can respect you
And see you at your best.

Verse 10

'This is a rule of friendship:
Dogs play with those they respect.
When you can block a bully,
It's much easier to connect.

Verse 11

'But if they are still mean or nasty,
Just go cold like ice.
Don't look at them or say a word,
Avoid them like they're lice.'

Verse 12

Mia *added,* 'Most dogs think that
Teasing is just like friendly banter.
They think it cannot threaten you
Or cause you to feel anger.

Verse 13

'Even when they tease and say,
"Come on, it's just a joke.
I wouldn't try to hurt you,
I'm really a nice bloke."

Verse 14

'But they do not realise
That bullying causes pain
And, if it goes on for too long,
Will actually harm your brain.

Verse 15

'When good friends ignore you,
Tease or banter, let them know
That you don't find it funny
And it upsets you so.

Verse 16

'What does their feedback really show?
Do they care or do they ignore?
Tell them you might walk away
And find others who care more.'

Chapter Six

Verse 17

Then Max the Maltese added,
'Little dogs can be excluded.
But we don't like that, so we bark
And ask to be included.

Verse 18

'When you speak to mean dogs,
Make sure they hear just what you say.
Your words should come out loud and clear —
Don't mumble, stutter or look away.

Verse 19

'Once they realise that
Their teases do not matter,
They won't bother you any more.
They will leave or start to chatter.'

Verse 20

Then Layla the Labrador said,
'Some dogs are really sensitive.
I'm one of them and, if bullied,
I can become very negative.

Verse 21

'But everyone likes playing with
Dogs who are content and calm,
Not pushy, sad or angry.
A good mood works like a charm.'

Chapter Six

Verse 22

Then Layla the Labrador continued:
'If you're sick of the teasing
Don't let those meanies get you down –
Become a friendly, social being.

Verse 23

'Most dogs are nice to me
Because I smile and wag my tail.
They know they will have fun with me.
A kindly greeting cannot fail.'

Verse 24

She said, 'The best greeting is simple:
'You just need to say, "Hello".
Then smile and look them in the eye.
And let your friendly face show.

Verse 25

'They can see I'm interested
When I listen with a "noddie".
I make sure I'm not distracted
In my mind or in my body.

Verse 26

'I give them my full attention
Not like kids with a phone,
Who act like they don't care,
But don't want to be alone.

Chapter Six

Verse 27

'I always have four questions
That work for girls and boys.
I ask about their favourite things,
Like friends, sports, apps and toys.

Verse 28

'I have good friends partly because
I ask interesting questions.
I show them care and, at times,
I make some kind suggestions.

Verse 29

'Dogs like dogs who care,
And we've enjoyed helping you.
So if you like what you've been told,
You can help others, too.

Verse 30

'Ask your mates for help and say,
"Don't be bully bystanders.
We should stick together
And be good bully up-standers!"

Verse 31

'So when you see a dog alone,
Don't let them stay excluded.
Use what you've learnt here today
And make sure they're included.'

Chapter Seven

Verse 1

Suddenly, Harry woke up!
He was cold and hungry.
He'd been sleeping for so long
Under the old camellia tree.

Verse 2

It was time to go inside
And eat some yummy food,
Play with Buffy and then
Go to sleep in a good mood.

Verse 3

Next day, he went back to puppy school.
As he walked upon the grass,
He looked around and there they were:
The mean dogs from his class.

Verse 4

He remembered to act cool and calm -
His worries are his alone.
The mean dogs want him scared;
His fears must not be shown!

Verse 5

He stood straight, with good eye-contact,
And wore a nice, square smile.
He didn't shake or jump around,
Just used a neutral style.

Verse 6

When they started teasing him,
His retorts were simple and clear.
He remembered some wise words, and said,
'Fancy that!' 'Really?' 'Oh dear!'

Verse 7

What happened next was that
Harry checked the bullies' feedback.
He was worried they'd be angry
After his neutral comeback.

Verse 8

But they looked stunned and surprised,
They couldn't even scoff.
After Harry blocked them,
They were quiet and just moved off.

Chapter Seven

Verse 9

He knew at once that it had worked:
Those doggies were dismayed.
They had no answer to
The clever game that he had played!

Verse 10

Harry didn't react while they were there
But smiled when off they went.
He felt proud and strong -
In a word, really content!

Verse 11

His parents were so proud of him
And his simple stunt.
He got a special treat that night
And gave a happy grunt.

Verse 12

Dogs don't use social media,
But some bullies do.
And there too Harry's bully blockers
Work just like Kung Fu.

Verse 13

Remember when Harry felt sad, mad or bad?
Now that he's a bully blocker,
Those tough times are over because
No one acts improper.

Verse 14

He fills his playtime with good friends.
He is kind but still assertive.
He is friendly but no pushover,
And his mates are most supportive.

Verse 15

Harry still makes mistakes sometimes
But says, 'No need for fits:
Everything will be all right.
What can I learn from this?'

Verse 16

So if you are ever bullied,
Now or when you're older,
Remember Harry and his friends
And act a little bolder.

Verse 17

Just regard this as a game:
Don't make those bullies happy
By acting like they bother you
And being scared or snappy.

Verse 18

Look them straight in the eye
And put on a blank face.
Or, if you'd rather not look at them,
Just stare into space.

Verse 19

If they are being mean to you,
Just say 'And?' 'What?' or 'Thanks.'
Use a neutral comeback like this
Or have fun using word pranks.

Verse 20

And remember, everybody likes
A friendly, caring face.
If you wear one, you might see
Some magic taking place!

Verse 21

You don't have to play alone -
Find friendly dogs you know.
Do some 'noddies', add a smile,
And watch your social life grow.

Chapter Seven

Verse 22

Now, when Harry goes to bed at night,
He's happy, without doubt.
We all know this for sure because
His little tongue peeps out!

The End

End of Book Exercises

Author note:

When one of my grandchildren suddenly hid under the table after I read aloud a few chapters of *Harry the Bully Blocker*, I realised this story can bring up very sad, painful feelings for a bullied child. It is therefore an excellent starting point for an important discussion between a parent or therapist and the child about dealing with bullying — as well as developing vital social skills.

Chapter 1

Verse 3	What kinds of things do children feel upset about?
Verse 6	What does it mean to be shy?
Verse 6	What are some things that make you scared?
Verse 7	Is there something you feel bad about that gives you constant grief, like Harry? Why?
Verse 9	Do you ever push friendly children away? If so, why?

Chapter 2

Verse 1	What mean words do you hear at your school?
Verse 5	Do kids who are different get bullied at your school?
Verse 6	How does a target make it easy for bullies to pick on him/her?
Verse 8	Can anyone hide their feelings, even to dogs?
Verse 9	What does 'toughen up' mean? Can you do this, or is it too hard?
Verse 11	Do you ever feel bad about yourself as a person?

Chapter 3

Verse 7 'This question startled young Harry,
Whose eyebrows rose and ears wiggled.
He gasped for air and looked at her.
She smiled when his nose jiggled!'

Can you show me how you do this?

Verse 14	How do bullies smell stress?
Verse 15	What is the gut instinct?
Verse 16	What do others see us doing when we feel angry, scared or stunned?
Verse 17	What was Harry's false belief?

Chapter 4

Verse 3	What is a better way to express your feelings when you are angry, scared or sad?
Verse 5	Why is eye-contact so important? Show me how you do it.
Verse 7	Can you sit still and be quiet? Show me.
Verse 10	Can you stand or sit up straight and look confident? Show me.
Verse 13	Why is your brain so smart? How can you use your smart brain to manage your worries?
Verse 14	Can you show me how you make a cool, calm or blank face?
Verse 17	How do you behave around dogs or children who don't care about you?
Verse 23	How do your friends protect you, and how can you protect your friends?

Exercises

Chapter 5

Verse 2   What other teases are common at your school?

Verse 3   Do the mean children you know use many teases, or just a few?

Verse 7   Why do we get upset at teases that are true, and at teases that are not true?

Verse 11   What else can children do to reduce the teasing, e.g. practise sport at home?

Verse 12   Here are some examples of comebacks for when you agree, disagree or are neutral: 'Thanks for telling me', 'It's genetic', 'I'm not stupid, I just have some learning problems',
'Life is tough', 'Thanks for the feedback.'

Can you think of some other examples?

Verse 15   What is a good reply? Can you make up some other replies to the mean things children say to you at school or elsewhere?

Chapter 6

Verse 4   What does 'hitting the bull's-eye' mean?

Verse 6   Can you show me how you look when your eyes open wide, your jaw opens wide, and you do a quick headshake? Is it funny?

Verse 7   Can you show me how you look when you feel embarrassed?

Verse 8   Why don't children like being embarrassed?

Verse 18	How do you speak clearly and loudly, in a natural way, e.g. like in front of a TV camera?
Verse 20	Why do most children prefer to avoid sensitive or negative children?
Verse 25	Show me how you look friendly and do a 'noddie'.
Verse 26	How do you show interest in another person?
Verse 27	What are 3-5 questions you could ask a friend to show them you are interested?
Verse 31	How can you include other children in your games and activities?

Chapter 7

Verse 5	Do you know what a 'square smile' is? Show me.
Verse 7	Feedback is what others say and do to you. How do you get it?
Verse 7	What is a neutral comeback? How does it take power away from the bully?
Verse 10	Why shouldn't you smile when mean children get an embarrassed look on their face?
Verse 14	Why are Harry's friends supportive?
Verse 17	What can you do instead of being scared or snappy?

Verse 19 A word prank is a game with words.
For example:
Bully says, 'Carrot tops.' You reply,
'No, they're actually green.'
Or Bully says, 'You're dumb.' You reply,
'Then why can I talk?'
Or Bully says, 'No one likes you.' You reply,
'My family really care about me.'

Can you think of any others?

Verse 20 Why will magic take place?

Verse 22 How do you show that you are happy?

Notes for parents and teachers for involving children in further discussion

1. Ask children how they identify feelings in themselves and others.
2. Write down some options, e.g. What can Harry do or say now?
3. What do you think will happen next?
4. Have you ever felt like Harry or the other dogs in the story?
5. Do you know children who are similar to Harry or the other dogs?
6. If you were a bystander, what could you think, say or do?
7. When you become a bully blocker, why do most children respect you, and some children want to play with you?

Acknowledgements

I want to thank Sean Doyle, who transformed a clumsy manuscript into a magical therapy poem.

I also want express my gratitude to the Australian Psychological Society for enabling me to provide years of training to its members.

Thanks, too, to the following for their helpful feedback:

Jude Bergman	Estelle Fookes	George from PO Jewel
Brett Bedson	Nicole Goldhammer	Isobel Morgan
Kathy Deutch	Greta Grossberg	Sandy Sable
Judith David	Emma Kranz	Vivien, Stephanie's mother
Anna Field	David Opat	Vivian Rich
Pam Fradkin	Carrie Parrott	

For more information about bullying, Evelyn's other books and many further resources, please visit Evelyn's website:

www.bullying.com.au

Harry the Bully Blocker – the audiobook

Paul Archer, composer of the music for the audiobook, says of the project:

'It has been a pleasure to write the music for *Harry the Bully Blocker*. Harry, a beloved pet of Evelyn's, called for me to musically represent his playful and kind nature, as well as underscore his narrative journey in this wonderful audiobook. Evelyn's suggestion to fuse Eastern elements into the music score proved a masterstroke. The ehru, a two-stringed Chinese instrument, proved the perfect voice for Harry, offering an expressive and at times very vulnerable sound. The harp forms a wonderful sonic bridge between Eastern and Western tonalities, and has a beautifully delicate quality — perfect for the score. Other instruments featured include strings, flute and bassoon as well as the shakuhachi (Chinese); the gayageum, jeongak and janggu (Korean); and a small section with taiko drums (Japanese) in the finale.

Harry the Bully Blocker addresses an important issue. It has been my honour to be on board with this project. My humble thanks to Evelyn and Sean for their support.'

You can access the audiobook of *Harry the Bully Blocker* — featuring a soothing reading voice and lovely ambient music — via Evelyn's website:

www.bullying.com.au

CPSIA information can be obtained
at www.ICGtesting.com
Printed in the USA
BVHW021751170222
629333BV00021B/586